The Real World?

THE REAL WORLD?

Michel Tremblay

Talonbooks　　•　　Vancouver　　•　　1988

copyright ©1988 Michel Tremblay

translation copyright ©1988 John Van Burek and
Bill Glassco

published with assistance from the Canada Council

Talonbooks
201/1019 East Cordova Street
Vancouver, British Columbia
Canada V6A 1M8

This book was typeset in Garth by Pièce de Résistance
Graphics, and printed by Hignell Printing Ltd.

Printed in Canada

First printing: October 1988

First published by Les Editions Leméac Inc., Montréal,
Québec.

Canadian Cataloguing in Publication Data

Tremblay, Michel, 1943-
  [Le vrai monde? English]
  The real world?

  Translation of: Le vrai monde?
  ISBN 0-88922-260-6

  I. Title.   II. Title: Le vrai monde?
English.
PS8539.R47V713 1988   C842'.54   C88-091495-5
PQ3919.2.T73V713 1988

Le Vrai Monde? was first performed at le Théâtre du Rideau Vert in Montréal, Québec, on April 15, 1987, with the following cast:

Madeleine II	Angèle Coutu
Madeleine I	Rita Lafontaine
Claude	Patrice Coquereau
Alex I	Gilles Renaud
Alex II	Raymond Bouchard
Mariette I	Sylvie Ferlatte
Mariette II	Julie Vincent

Directed by André Brassard
Assisted by Lou Fortier
Costumes by François Barbeau
Set Design by Martin Ferland
Lighting by Claude Accolas

The Real World? was first performed in English at Tarragon Theatre in Toronto, Ontario, on May 24, 1988, with the following cast:

Madeleine II	Shirley Douglas
Madeleine I	Clare Coulter
Claude	Michael McManus
Alex I	Graeme Campbell
Alex II	Ken James
Mariette I	Julie A. Stewart
Mariette II	Shannon Lawson

Directed by Bill Glassco
Costumes by François Barbeau
Set Design by André Henault
Lighting by Jeffrey Dallas

The living room is empty.
We hear the third movement of Mendelsohn's fifth
symphony.
MADELEINE II enters; she seems troubled.
She goes to the door, pulls the curtain, and looks
outside.
She crosses the living room again and goes out.
We hear a popular song from the mid-sixties.

CLAUDE and ALEX I enter. CLAUDE carries a
leather briefcase, his father a small suitcase.

CLAUDE:
Looks like you never left the dirt roads. I've never
seen such a filthy car . . .

ALEX I:
Nonsense! When you were a kid, my car was always
that dirty . . . There weren't many paved roads in the
forties . . . But of course, you don't notice things like
that . . . You've always got your nose buried in
books, how would you know what my car looks
like . . .

MADELEINE I comes in from the kitchen. She is
dressed like MADELEINE II, but simpler, more
"realistically."

MADELEINE I:
Home already, Alex? I didn't expect you 'til
tomorrow . . .   *She is visibly uneasy; coldly:*
Hello, Claude . . .

CLAUDE:
Hi . . .

He kisses his mother awkwardly.

ALEX I:
Gee, I can tell you're thrilled to see me . . . No kiss for hubby? You haven't seen me for a whole week. Claude, you see him almost every day . . . worry about him later . . .

He lifts her off the ground, gives her a big kiss on the cheek.

MADELEINE I:
Alex, for God's sake . . .

ALEX I:
Mmmm, smells good . . . I mean . . . you smell good, the whole house smells good . . .

MADELEINE I:
Life goes on, even when you're away.

She goes out.

ALEX I:
Something happen while I was gone?

CLAUDE:
I don't know . . . don't think so . . . Anyway, I haven't been here for at least a week . . . I don't hang around all the time . . .

ALEX I:
It wasn't that way when you moved out . . . You always came home to eat with your mother . . .

CLAUDE:
That was two years ago . . .

ALEX I:
Two years! Already! You sure?

CLAUDE:
Believe it or not, I've learned how to cook myself a steak, and the peas that go with it . . .

Silence.

ALEX I:
So, how's the new job?

CLAUDE:
It's okay.

ALEX I:
That's all you've got to say?

CLAUDE:
Listen, Papa, I've got the most boring job in the
world. Just because it's a new one doesn't make it any
better.

ALEX I:
If you'd listened to me . . .

CLAUDE:
Oh please, let's not start that again . . . We've been
over this a hundred times, it's pointless . . . I have no
interest in roaming the countryside year in, year out,
flogging insurance with a smile on my face and a
hatful of jokes . . . especially under the protection of
my famous father . . . Can you see us two travelling
together? We'd have killed each other in two weeks!

ALEX I:
You'd be on your own in no time . . . build your own
clientele, like me.

CLAUDE:
Papa, please, you're giving me the creeps!

ALEX I:
Well I still think you'd be happier that way than
spending your life strapped to a machine that drives
you nuts . . . And you'd see the country! At least I've
spent my life in the open air. And I've had fun! I'm
not bored up the ass eight hours a day in some
printing shop that stinks to high heaven!

CLAUDE:
> I won't be strapped to that machine much longer . . .

ALEX I:
> You still dream of being a writer. You make a living, but you're stuck in a job you don't like . . . and you dream of starving to death in a job that'll never support you . . . I'll never understand you . . .

CLAUDE:
> What else is new . . .

> *ALEX I looks at his son for a few seconds. We can feel the tension mount.*

ALEX I:
> You still carry your little briefcase, like an intellectual? What do you keep in there? Your lunch?   *CLAUDE lowers his eyes.*   Your lunch and your manuscripts . . . When can we expect the great revelation? Eh? The third Tuesday next month? Mind you, if it's poetry, don't bother. I get enough of that from those jerks plunking their guitars in every hotel in the province . . . How come all you people are plunking guitars all of a sudden? It's an epidemic! I just saw another one, Saturday night in Saint-Jérôme. Jesus-Christ, even Felix Leclerc's not that boring.

CLAUDE:
> Don't worry . . . What I write about has nothing to do with guitars . . .

ALEX I:
> That's a relief . . . I guess.   *He laughs.*   I know you well enough to know that whatever you write isn't gonna make me do handstands . . .

CLAUDE:
> Then don't ask me why I don't show it to you . . .

MADELEINE I returns clutching a manuscript.
CLAUDE turns away slightly.

ALEX I:
A roast of veal? A chicken?

MADELEINE I:
Roast of veal.   *Ironically.*   Claude's so fond of
that . . .

ALEX I: *to CLAUDE*
That reminds me . . . Go look in the trunk of the
car . . . I've got a whole bag of corn . . . first of the
year . . . It's beautiful, it's young, it's tender . . . Just
like me!

MADELEINE I rolls her eyes to heaven.

MADELEINE I:
Spare us the travelling salesman jokes . . .

ALEX I:
It's my travelling salesman jokes that pay for your
roast of veal, Madeleine!   *MADELEINE I and*
CLAUDE look at each other.   Okay, I'm going to
take a bath . . . I've a hunch I smell like team
work . . .   *He laughs.*   Don't miss me too
much . . .

He goes out.
Silence.
MADELEINE I lays the manuscript on the coffee
table.

CLAUDE:
Have you read it?

MADELEINE I:
Yes.   *Silence.*   How could you do that . . . ? I
was so ashamed reading it, Claude . . . I felt so . . .
ugly.

CLAUDE:
Ugly?

MADELEINE I: *sharply*
That's not me! That's not how I am! That woman,
even if she has my name, is nothing like me! And I
don't want her to be. How dare you give her my
name, Claude!

CLAUDE:
But Mama, it's a character in a play . . . Nothing says
it's you . . .

MADELEINE I:
Claude! What do you take me for? You describe our
living room down to the last detail! The furniture, the
curtains, the frayed carpet in front of the door, the
Admiral T.V . . . It takes place right here, in our
house, how do you expect me not to think you
wanted to describe us in those characters! I
recognized my dress, Claude, I recognized my hairdo,
but I didn't recognize myself!

> *We hear the beginning of the third movement of*
> *Mendelsohn's fifth symphony.*
> *MADELEINE II enters; she seems troubled. She is*
> *dressed like MADELEINE I.*
> *MADELEINE I picks up the manuscript.*

MADELEINE I:
What's in here is not me!

> *MADELEINE II goes to the window, pulls the*
> *curtains and looks out.*

MADELEINE I:
That's not me!

> *MADELEINE II crosses the room again in silence,*
> *and goes out.*

MADELEINE I:
> That's not even the music I listen to! The music you
> put in there, I don't know it. And I don't want to! The
> music I listen to is simple, it's easy to remember, I can
> sing along with it. You hear what's playing on the
> kitchen radio? Well, that's what I like. Not your . . .
> your . . .

CLAUDE:
> Mendelsohn . . .

MADELEINE I:
> Your Mendelsohn that you've found God knows
> where . . . from your own taste probably . . . Were
> you ashamed to put that in your play? I can't
> understand what you were after! You've made us all
> ugly, but you've made us listen to music you think is
> more beautiful, more refined than what we like! You
> make fools of us, Claude, do you realize that?

CLAUDE:
> But I don't. I don't make fools of you. Come and sit
> next to me. I'll try to explain . . .

MADELEINE I:
> I don't want explanations, it's too late for that, the
> harm's been done! You have no idea how much
> you've hurt me . . .   *Silence.*   How can you
> think . . . that I ever thought such things, that I ever
> said . . . such monstrous things to your father!

CLAUDE:
> I know you never said them . . . that's why I wrote
> them. Mama, there are things in this house that
> should have been dealt with a long time ago, that
> have never been settled . . .

MADELEINE I:
> Who are you to decide what's to be settled between
> your father and me . . .

ALEX II enters with an enormous bouquet of flowers.

ALEX II:
Madeleine! Madeleine, are you there?

CLAUDE:
That's not what I was trying to do . . . I wasn't trying to settle them, but I wanted those things to be said once and for all.

MADELEINE II comes back in, her arms folded across her chest, like the real MADELEINE.

MADELEINE II:
I've been waiting for you for two days. Flowers won't settle a thing.

ALEX II:
Okay, what is it this time . . . You know I had a long way to go . . .

MADELEINE II looks him straight in the eye.

MADELEINE II:
Alex, I know exactly where you've been . . .

ALEX II:
What's that supposed to mean? I told you, this time I might have to go all the way to Sept Îsles . . . Sept Îsles, Madeleine, that's not next door!

MADELEINE II:
No, but Sorel is right around the corner, isn't it? *ALEX II is flummoxed. Silence.* Sept Îsles! I've known for ages you don't cover the whole province of Quebec by yourself. In the beginning . . . in the beginning, when I was young, I believed you, I thought you went everywhere, that you were the only one out there . . . I was even naive enough to think your company depended almost entirely on you. When you talked about your job you made yourself

14

sound so important, I was convinced that if you
disappeared your company'd go bankrupt . . . I loved
you that much . . .

ALEX II:
Why the past tense? You don't love me anymore? I
still love you . . .

She looks at him a few seconds before replying.

MADELEINE II:
Indeed, sometimes just to get through the day, I tell
myself you must love me, in your way.

ALEX II:
Madeleine, what's wrong with you lately, you seem
distant . . . but I've been telling myself it's not
serious, it'll pass . . .

MADELEINE II:
Alex, I really don't feel like listening to your
excuses . . . But . . . I'm fed up being taken for a
fool . . . I've started to take myself for a fool, and that,
Alex, I won't do . . .

ALEX II:
Excuses . . . for what?

MADELEINE II:
Everything! The lies, the cheating, the manipulation,
your specialty, which only I couldn't see . . . I
believed you for so long, and I was content to believe
you . . .

ALEX II:
For Chrissake, are you going to start accusing me too,
of always being happy! It's bad enough when the kids
make cracks all the time! Sure, I manipulate, sure, I
want people to like me, and sure, I do everything so
they will, but that doesn't make me a bastard!

MADELEINE II:

It's not people I want to talk about, Alex . . . You can do what you want with them, that's your job. It's your job to seduce them with your stupid jokes and dirty stories so they'll sign their names to a contract that's likely going to screw them.

ALEX II:

That's how you see my job . . .

MADELEINE II:

That's how you talk about it . . . You ever listen to yourself? You ever stop to think about the stupid things you say in one day? Jokes are fine, Alex, even dirty ones, but not all day long. When we were first married I said to myself, that's okay, he wants to make me laugh, it'll pass . . . until I realized you were always that way, and you probably always would be . . . I loved you too much to admit you got on my nerves . . . or I wanted to love you too much. I was the only one in the family to find something resembling love, and I did everything, everything I could not to lose it . . . I even stayed blind to what you were doing . . .

ALEX II:

But what did I do? All my life I've slaved for you and the kids . . . You've had nothing to complain about, never! Nobody has! Sure, I travelled a lot, but when I came home we had fun! We've had fun in this house for years, Madeleine, we don't kill each other like everyone else in your family, and you want to complain! Christ, does everyone in your family have to suffer? Would you rather I knocked you around after I'd had a few? Like your brother-in-law? When the kids were small their friends would love to have had me for a father, I was like Santa Claus with Mariette and Claude! Did you want me to be a boogie man they'd run away from when I got home? I gave those kids presents, Madeleine, not bruises! I came back to town like a ray of sunshine, and the whole damn street was happy to see me! Everyone envied you, so don't tell me I made you miserable!

MADELEINE II:

Alex, I know you've got answers for everything . . . That's why I avoid these arguments . . . You're a smooth talker, that's how you make your living and put food on the table, you know how to control a conversation . . . Next to you we're helpless, defenceless . . . We let you win because even if we argue for hours sooner or later you'll get us with some devious trick or joke . . . See, you've turned the conversation already. I was determined to try and talk to you calmly, to tell you calmly that I know what you've done to me, and you've got me all mixed up already . . . I feel like going back to the kitchen to finish supper, pretending I know nothing, that I'm ignorant and happy again! No question, I was better off when I knew nothing, when my world stopped at the doorstep, and my only worries were that the kids eat properly and be well dressed, and for you to be proud of us when you came home . . . No question . . . When you know nothing, you can't be hurt . . . See that door? . . . That's where my world stopped, Alex, and I was perfectly happy. Perfectly! For . . . I don't know, twenty years. When you were out of my sight, you vanished into thin air, almost ceased to exist . . . You became . . . I don't know . . . Prince Charming on a promotional tour . . . I knew you were off playing the clown to put food in our mouths, but since I never saw you at it, I could imagine whatever I liked. For me you were someone important . . . I admired you! *She sits on the sofa next to MADELEINE I.* Now I'm caught in the middle of a scene I didn't plan, and I don't know how to continue.

MADELEINE I:

Did you ever consider, Claude, that I'm too proud to admit such things . . . I'd rather die than say those things to your father.

ALEX II:

I've always admired you too . . . *MADELEINE II*
stiffens on the sofa. No, no let me finish . . .

MADELEINE II:

No, Alex . . . I know what you're going to say and I
don't want to fall into the trap . . . I'd rather keep you
from talking than let myself be fooled again . . .

ALEX II:

I don't have the right to speak in my own house? Is
that it? You're so afraid of being wrong, you're going
to keep me from talking! For once I'm about to pay
you compliments, real ones, heartfelt, and you're
going to plug your ears!

MADELEINE II:

I don't want your admiration, Alex. It's
contemptuous! You admire me like a statue on a
shelf, like a tin of Campbell's soup that's handy when
you get hungry before bed! You don't admire me, you
appreciate the fact I'm always here to wait on you
when you come home, that's all. For you this house
has never been more than a train station. You only
come here waiting to leave again. Convenient, eh?
While you were out gallivanting around the province
you could always be sure there were three saps
waiting patiently, keeping your meals hot, your bed
clean, and your slippers under your armchair!

ALEX II:

I don't recognize you . . .

MADELEINE II:

I hope not! And I tell you, it'll be a while before you
do.

ALEX II:
>Listen . . . Let's just calm down . . . I come home happy, with a bouquet of flowers that cost me an arm and a leg . . . We haven't seen each other for over a week . . . I'm eager to get home . . . I walk in, and I find another woman!

MADELEINE II:
>Ahah! That's exactly what I wanted to talk about. Thank you. You got us back on the subject without meaning to . . . another woman!

>*MADELEINE I gets up.*

MADELEINE I: *very sharply*
>You've got nerve! Making up stories like that just to be interesting! Your father's right. You've always had a . . . warped imagination . . .

CLAUDE:
>You'd rather let Papa be right than admit the truth . . .

MADELEINE I:
>What truth? Yours? One that you fancy because it's more interesting for your play?

CLAUDE:
>Mama . . . there's no point pretending you don't know about Papa . . . Mariette and I have known the truth about him for ages . . .

MADELEINE I:
>Well, keep it to yourself! Don't put it on paper! Someone might read it! I don't even admit those things to myself; how do you expect me to tolerate finding them in some play! Now I've read that, I'll never be able to look at your father in the same way. Never thought of that, did you, you just wanted to smear him! To smear us! That scene about other women never took place, and it never will, you hear

me? As long as I live I'll keep that scene from
happening!

CLAUDE:
I hoped it would do you good . . .

MADELEINE I:
Well, it didn't! It revived something in me that I'd
buried forever. Forever, Claude! You've brought
back . . . the one thing that almost drove me
insane . . . doubt. Thanks to you, I've started to doubt
again, and I'll never forgive you!

She leaves the room.

MADELEINE II:
I've never talked to you . . . about other women . . .

ALEX II:
What other women?

MADELEINE II:
Alex, please, don't make this more difficult . . . it's
hard enough already. Let's not play games. Everyone
in the house knows, Alex. We always have.

ALEX II:
Why do we have to talk about this . . . ?

MADELEINE II:
To get it off my chest, maybe.

ALEX II:
I don't want to talk about these things. It's
embarrassing. They're unimportant anyway. Women
have always attracted me, you know that . . . I never
denied it . . .

MADELEINE II:
You're telling me . . . Every year at Christmas I was
terrified . . . A woman couldn't make it through the
door without you lunging at her.

ALEX II:

> Come off it, Madeleine! Sure, after a few drinks, I'd
> get a bit enterprising, but so did all the men!

MADELEINE II:

> Sure, with you guys it's always the same. Without a
> drink you're shy as calves, but once you've tanked
> up, any woman's fair game! Christmas, weddings,
> First Communions, any excuse for a party! A few
> drinks and you can't keep your hands off, that's your
> idea of a party! You don't even try to hide it when
> you're pawing your sisters-in-law or your young
> cousins. You do it in front of everyone too, roaring
> away, making lewd jokes just to show it's not serious.
> 'Course not! As long as it doesn't go too far, eh? The
> drinks give you the freedom to carry on, but you
> know you can't go too far. Meanwhile we poor girls
> sit there like idiots laughing our heads off 'cause we
> don't know what else to do. Because we're so
> ashamed. We're ashamed of you guys, so we laugh!
> But it's not men in general I want to talk about, it's
> you, about what you've been doing all these years
> while you were gone; about what I bet you're still
> doing, that's what I want to talk about . . .

ALEX II:

> What I do when I go out that door is my business,
> Madeleine. If something happens at the other end of
> the province, what do you care? Look, I'm a
> red-blooded man, I've got needs. Sometimes I'm gone
> for weeks, and . . . there are women for that,
> Madeleine, and you know it! But it's not serious. It
> doesn't stop me feeling what I feel for you. And I've
> never let you down, I've always . . . When I come
> home, Madeleine, you can't say . . . I don't know
> how to talk about these things! What you don't know
> won't hurt you, why do you want to know
> everything?

MADELEINE II:

I know enough already, thank you, and it hurts! I've got my pride too, you know! You can't walk all over me like that and not expect me to feel something! You've been laughing at me since the day we got married, Alex. I've had enough!

ALEX II:

I don't laugh at you!

MADELEINE II:

You're laughing at me right now! Because you've no idea how much I know . . . Because you hope I don't know everything! Well, let me tell you a story. Just one, to show you what I've put up with . . . One day someone knocked at the door . . . I opened it. It was a woman, with a little girl in her arms. You know what I'm talking about?   *ALEX II turns away.*   She said her name was Madame Cantin . . . Does that ring a bell, Alex, Madame Cantin . . . from Sorel?

ALEX II:

She came here?

MADELEINE II:

Years ago. She told me she hadn't seen you for months, that you'd left her without a cent . . .

ALEX II:

You've known each other for years and neither one of you ever told me!

MADELEINE II:

We have our little secrets too, you know . . . How old is she now, that little girl? Must be a teenager. Don't worry, we don't get together behind your back. I don't even know her phone number. But I know she exists, and that's what kills me! Can you imagine how I felt giving her ten dollars out of my purse? Eh? The humiliation! For her as much as for me! Behind the clown, the joker, the professional smoothie, there's a man I don't know, who leads a double life I don't

know, and who probably cheats on this second
woman with yet a third . . . Is there an end, is there
any end, Alex, to your cheating? Have you sown your
oats in every city you've worked in? Is there a
Madame Cantin in Sept Îsles, another in
Drummondville? Do they all have trouble feeding
your kids? Madame Cantin called from Sorel this
afternoon, Alex . . . Once again you "forgot" to leave
her some money . . . And I can't live with this lie any
longer.

ALEX II:
That kid's probably not even mine! I got taken for a
ride, what else could I do? She meant no more than
the others at first, but . . . but one day she said I'd got
her pregnant and I believed her . . . I should have
dropped her then and there 'cause she'd known lots
of men before me, and nothing says that kid was
mine . . . But . . . you, you didn't want any more
kids, and I felt like it . . . it made me feel good to have
another one . . .

MADELEINE II:
Sure, keep it up, it'll be my fault . . .

ALEX II: *cutting her off*
And I've always assumed my responsibilities . . .

MADELEINE II:
You left her repeatedly with no money!

ALEX II:
I didn't have any! It was hard enough feeding the rest
of you. I was up against it, Madeleine. There were
times I left you without money too! If I didn't have
enough for you, how could I give her any? And there
aren't any others, at Sept Îsles or Drummondville.
She's the only one . . .

MADELEINE II:
You mean she's the only one with kids . . .

23

ALEX II:

> Some guys should never get married. I found out too
> late I was one of them . . .

MADELEINE II:

> Boy, you sure solve problems fast! Is that why you
> dumped us in the backwoods every summer from
> June to September, and gave us the thrill of your
> presence once in a blue moon . . . You carried on like
> you weren't even married! One helluva life, eh! Every
> year, three months off to go chase skirts! A month
> here, a month there . . . Do you tell them all the same
> thing when they question you? Do you? Do you say
> it's me who's not important, or do I have the honour
> of being queen-mother?

ALEX II:

> What am I supposed to say! You think I was happy all
> those years . . . ?

MADELEINE II:

> Hey, don't expect me to feel sorry for you!

ALEX II:

> Will you let me talk! Okay, it's true . . . I like to sow
> my oats, as you put it . . . But for me it's not
> important . . . It's just . . . it's just a need, it's
> natural . . . something I happen to feel when I'm
> alone on a Saturday night, stuck in some gloomy
> hotel . . . And if it weren't for that kid . . .

MADELEINE II:

> If it weren't for that kid I'd never have known and
> things would have gone on like before 'til the end of
> time, right? Deep down inside, that's your dream,
> isn't it? To be Mr. Wonderful with me while you
> laugh behind my back, as you skip from town to
> town, woman to woman, knowing I'll always be here
> in my fool's paradise, in blissful ignorance, with my
> roast of beef and my apple pie! And in spite of
> everything, that's what I cooked yesterday, a roast of
> beef and an apple pie . . . because that's what you

like . . . But the roast dried up and I couldn't resist the pie. There are two pieces missing . . .

She holds her sides.

ALEX II:
You what's wrong? You in pain again?

ALEX II:
What's wrong? You in pain again?

MADELEINE II:
I can deal with my own pain, thank you . . . Never mind the sympathy. It'll get you no further than your stupid jokes. Now that you know everything, no need to tell you I don't want to go on. I'll never find you funny again, and if you only knew how good that makes me feel! I'll do everything possible to get a divorce, Alex. Even though I know it's going to be long and hard. In the mean time, while you're in Montreal you can find yourself a gloomy hotel; that way you can be sure you won't be bored on Saturday nights . . .

She goes out.
Silence.
ALEX II goes to the telephone.

ALEX II:
Goddamnit! She'll pay for that!

He goes out with the telephone.
MADELEINE I enters.
She is holding a glass of milk.

CLAUDE:
You in pain again?

MADELEINE I:
You had no business talking about that either. But I suppose there's no point telling you that. There's just one thing I want you to know, Claude. I won't stay long, I'm going to disappear into my kitchen, as I always do. It's a roast of veal this time, just to be different from your play . . . but don't worry, there's

an apple pie . . .   *Silence*   I want to tell you
about something you left out of your play . . . silence.

CLAUDE:

I know what you're going to say about silence,
Mama . . .

MADELEINE I:

Well, listen anyway. Then, if you quote me again, at
least you'll get it right.   *She places herself very close
to her son.*   You see, in a house like this, it's the
most important thing. It's the only reason the walls
are still standing. Sure, it's true, when your father's
been gone for days and your sister's at work, I get
lonesome. I walk around the house, I don't know
what to do with myself . . . Television is boring and
I've never been a reader . . . I'm past the age when I
have to go out every day, even if it's just for a quart of
milk we don't need . . . So, without fail, I find myself
here, on the sofa, my hands folded on my knees and a
glass of milk on the coffee table in case my pains start
again . . . The first few minutes are always
difficult . . . Every day . . . It's terrifying, my
stomach's in a knot, I don't know how I'm going to
get through the next minute, how I'll survive the
afternoon that's hardly begun . . . Sometimes I'm
paralysed with fear . . . No, that's not right, it's not
fear. I'm not afraid something will happen to me, I
know nothing will happen, nothing! But I'm terrified
because I think I'm going to die from boredom. I've
got nothing to do. If I know your father's not coming
home then I just have a small meal to fix for Mariette
and myself, around six o'clock . . . and if Mariette
calls to say she won't be home, I'm fine with a can of
soup or a sandwich . . .   *Silence. We can sense how
troubled she is.*   So I have . . . five hours to fill. In
silence. And then, in the midst of the silence, the
storm breaks. I feel it coming . . . Sometimes I don't
want it to because I'm too tired or because my side
hurts, but it comes anyway . . . because I need it,
maybe . . . to pass the time. And then . . . it's true
that everything you put in your play goes through my

26

head . . . I told you earlier they were things I'd never
admit to myself . . . Of course, that's not true. I'm not
crazy, I know what my life's been like. So, I make up
scenes that go on for hours, scenes that are so violent,
you can't imagine . . . I throw off my burden, then I
take it on again . . . I become . . . some kind of
heroine . . . I wreck the house or I burn it down, I
slaughter your father, even worse than that . . . I
throw fits with you and your sister . . . Everything I
wouldn't dare say to you on the phone or when
you're here, comes out. It comes out in waves higher
than the house. But it all takes place in silence,
Claude. If you were to walk in in the middle of it,
you'd swear I was daydreaming or just planning
tonight's supper . . . because that's the image of
myself I always present . . . That's my strength. It's
always been that. Silence. I know nothing about
theatre, but I'll bet it's tough to do that, a storm in
somebody's head! But I'll tell you this much, it's a lot
more effective than some domestic brawl. Because it
does no harm. I've always put up with things in
silence because I know in the long run it pays off.
When you barricade yourself in there, you can think
whatever you like, even while doing something
completely different, and that gives others the
impression you want . . . Anyway, what would I gain
by doing like you say in your play? If I got a divorce,
where would I go? To be bored somewhere else? In
some dingy apartment for fools like me who didn't
have the sense to shut up? Find myself a job? All I can
do is cook and clean house. I'm not about to spend the
rest of my days cleaning house for rich people just
because once I got things off my chest! And I won't go
on having these afternoon nightmares in some two-bit
furnished apartment! That woman there in your play,
who bears my name and who's dressed like me,
what's she going to do the morning after? Eh? After
she's played the heroine? You couldn't care less about
that! When she opens the door and leaves the stage,
she doesn't exist anymore, and you couldn't care less,
as long as you've written some wonderful scenes! But
me, I have to go on living tomorrow, and the day after

tomorrow, and the day after that. If you've never heard the roar of my silence, Claude, you're not a real writer! *Silence.* You've got nothing to say. Admit it, that's not at all what you thought I'd say about silence . . .

CLAUDE:
Yes . . . I admit it. It's true, I didn't see you like that. But I still think your silence is unhealthy. You can't spend a whole lifetime in silence . . .

MADELEINE I:
Yes, you can.

CLAUDE:
A while ago you mentioned your pride . . . You said you were too proud to talk about those things with Papa . . . But your silence, Mama, isn't that humiliating too? It's all very well to sit here and blow off steam in your head, but isn't it humiliating to be an accomplice to everything he's done to you in your life? He's taking a bath, we heard him singing . . . Doesn't his presence insult you? Doesn't his vulgarity, his loud-mouthed, back-slapping grossness, make you shudder? Wouldn't it be more satisfying to go stand over him in his bath and tell him you've known everything all along, that you've nothing but contempt for him?

MADELEINE I:
It's you that needs to do that, Claude. It's your own problems with him you've put in your play, not mine. And I'll tell you something that'll make you shudder. You're unfair to him!

CLAUDE:
Mama!

MADELEINE I:
That's right, unfair!

CLAUDE:
You mean that scene with

MADELEINE I:
I mean everything! You've made
someone who's just a poor insignifi
insignificant, who tells off-colour joke
fact he's not too bright. He has an unbeli
memory for bad jokes, but it helps him thin
somebody! That's all. He's not even mean! Su
likes women, he travels and there's every
opportunity . . . but has it ever occured to you that
might suit me? For him to be far away, and have
others?

CLAUDE:
You're not being straight with me, now.

MADELEINE I:
You're right. At this point I'd tell you almost
anything, just to prove you're wrong.   *Sharply:*
It's true, I've always swallowed my pride, so what?
That doesn't give you the right to judge me.   *She
comes right up to CLAUDE.*   I'm all alone inside my
head, Claude, so I'm the only one who knows what I
think. Who are you to speak for me? The Messiah? I'll
save myself, thank you, I don't need you! And I
certainly don't need you to come along and make me
doubt myself! When I read your play, of course I was
shaken. I had doubts. About myself. I doubted I was
right. I saw myself here, in the living room, crucifying
your father, tearing a strip off him with a talent for
smart answers I've never had, and I told myself: what
a beautiful ending, what a splendid way to end it
all. But the consequences terrified me. I'd rather go
on imagining fabulous scenes that I can start and stop
whenever I like, than risk making a permanent mess
of a real one, for which I'd never forgive myself.
Silence.   I was so proud of you when you told me
you'd written a play. It's always thrilled me that you
wanted to be a writer . . . I encouraged you all I
could, even when the others teased you . . .

29

...n't tease me, they laughed at me!

MADELEINE I:

Fair enough . . . I said to myself . . . An artist in the family, a writer especially, that'll be a change . . . I'd never known anyone who wanted to be an artist. And all of a sudden there was one in my house! Not so long ago, when you were still living here, I'd find you asleep in your bed with a pencil and paper in your hands . . . You'd come home at night from your beatnik clubs, you'd grab a piece of paper and shut yourself up in your room for hours. It frightened me 'cause I thought the people you hung around with were dangerous . . . but still I was flattered . . . that here in my house there was someone who was interested in something other than hockey in winter and stupid baseball in summer! I'd found an ally to back me up at eight o'clock on Saturday night. Remember when you were small, when your father was home Saturday nights, the arguments we'd have because we wanted to see the movie on channel 6, even if it was in English, and your father and Mariette wanted to watch the hockey game? They'd always win and you'd slam the door to your room . . . and I knew what you were doing . . . You didn't ask me to read what you'd written and I didn't ask you to let me . . . I waited . . . I guess I waited for what happened this week . . . for that day when you'd come and say . . . ''Here, read this and tell me what you think . . . '' I was so proud! At last, a big pile of paper to read . . . I'd never seen a manuscript before. It didn't look like a book, but there was a chance it might become one . . . and . . . I was probably one of the first people to read it . . . before the publisher . . . before the printer . . . As soon as you left, I came in here and sat down . . . I was trembling, no kidding! I told myself . . . at last I'll know . . . what he's been cooking up all this time . . . I read the title . . . I wasn't too sure what it meant but that didn't matter . . . I read the names of the characters . . . I thought that was sweet of you to give our names to

30

characters in a play . . . you know . . . I'd never read
a play before and I wasn't too sure how it worked . . .
But . . . after a few pages . . . the deception . . . no,
worse than that . . . I don't know if there's a word to
describe what I felt . . . It was like a burning in my
stomach . . . like the dizziness you feel when you get
some terrible news . . . the betrayal! That's it, I felt
betrayed by my own son . . . I found my whole
life . . . disfigured . . . I could hear Mariette when
you were small, screaming at us that she'd caught you
in the corner again, spying on her . . . and I asked
myself . . . was she right all this time? Have I raised a
spy who copies down everything we say and do so he
can make fools of us later . . . ? Especially
because . . . when all's said and done, you don't
reveal yourself at all. That's what I want to talk to you
about. You talk about everyone in the family but
yourself. Oh, the others mention you, but you're not
there. Never. Why is that? I always thought writers
wrote about themselves . . . to explain
themselves . . . But you, you didn't even have the
courage to put yourself in your own play. By the end
of it, we have no idea who *you* are. You've made us
look horrible in there, you've arranged things to suit
yourself, as you see fit; you've even kept our names,
Claude, but you've hidden yourself. You stand
behind us and you tell the world: look how ugly they
are, how stupid . . .

CLAUDE:
I never said you were ugly or stupid. And if I didn't
talk about myself, it's 'cause I don't think I'm
interesting.

MADELEINE I:
Come off it! You've always done everything around
here to get attention, how come all of a sudden you're
not interesting? I'm more inclined to think it's
cowardice . . . You accuse your father all through the
play of being a coward, but you're no better . . . It's
hardly an act of courage, you know, to write a play
about people who can't defend themselves . . . How

31

are we supposed to answer back? All we can do is sit
here, submit to your attacks, put up with your lies,
because that's all they are, Claude, lies . . .

CLAUDE:
They're not lies, Mama. It's simply my way of seeing
things . . . It's one . . . version of the truth.

MADELEINE I:
Sure, a version you want to present in public while
we have to keep our version to ourselves!

CLAUDE:
You say you prefer silence . . . Well, I've decided to
speak . . .

MADELEINE I:
But not the truth! You've decided to speak for us,
Claude, who gave you that right? And your words are
the only ones that'll remain because they're the only
ones written down. You've no right to do that! No
right! Speak for yourself all you want, talk about
yourself, tell us your problems, but leave us alone. I
started out thinking I'd finally discover who my son
was, but all I found was . . . Ah, I'm not going to
repeat it again . . .

CLAUDE:
All writers do that, Mama. They take something they
know and they rework it as they see it . . .

MADELEINE I:
That's no excuse! I don't know the other writers and
they don't write lies about me. You're just getting in
deeper, Claude . . . Is it because you know you can't
answer me?

CLAUDE:
Mama . . . you don't know theatre . . .

MADELEINE I:

So why did you have me read it? You hand me a
mirror that distorts everything, then you tell me I
can't understand it.

CLAUDE:

On the contrary, I told you earlier I thought you'd
understand, that you'd appreciate what I tried to
do . . .

MADELEINE I:

Appreciate! Appreciate what? Your caricature? Your
contempt?

CLAUDE:

Contempt? You really feel contempt in my play? Even
for you?

MADELEINE I:

Yes.

CLAUDE:

For Papa, you're right . . . but for you and
Mariette . . . I really tried . . . with the best will in the
world . . . to defend you . . .

MADELEINE I:

I already told you . . . I don't need you to defend
me . . .

CLAUDE:

But what if I needed to defend you? If that was my
way of expressing myself? Through the rest of you?
Maybe it is spying, and maybe I used everything I
thought I knew about you all to say things that aren't
pretty to hear . . . that you don't want to hear . . . but
I do have the right! And you have to grant me that!

MADELEINE I:

No. No, I don't.

CLAUDE:
> Even if I act in good faith?

MADELEINE I:
> You can't act in good faith. Because you're not us . . .

CLAUDE:
> That's where you're wrong, Mama . . . Listen . . .
> Will you listen to me?   *MADELEINE I sits next to*
> *CLAUDE.*   It's always been very easy for me . . .
> to slip inside other people. To . . . feel them. I've
> always done that. The rest of you call it spying . . . I
> call it living. When I was in my corner watching you,
> listening to you, I was living intensely everything that
> was going on and everything that was being said. I'd
> record it in my mind, I'd recite it, afterwards I'd add
> things . . . I'd . . . I'd . . . It's true that after I'd
> correct it, what had happened . . . I'd become each
> one of you, I'd slide into each one of you and I'd try to
> understand . . . what it was like inside you . . .
> interpreting, sometimes changing what had
> happened . . . because sometimes what had
> happened wasn't revealing enough . . . That's what I
> still do . . . I try . . . I try to make sense of what goes
> on inside of other people . . .

MADELEINE I:
> And what goes on inside you doesn't interest you?

CLAUDE:
> I told you, I'm not interested in talking about that . . .

MADELEINE I:
> Well, I still say it's cowardice.

CLAUDE:
> Okay, fine . . . I see we can't talk about it . . . we're
> going in circles . . . repeating the same things to no
> end . . . I'm sorry I asked you to read it . . . If you
> like, I'll change the characters' names . . .

MADELEINE I:

What will that change for me? I've read it with my name. I've seen myself suffer in my own living room and say things I'd never say. It's too late! But there's another reason you asked me to read it . . . I know you . . .

CLAUDE:

We're going to put it on in a small theatre next fall, me and my friends.

MADELEINE I:

You're going to take that out of here? You're going to let people read that, perform it, play us? You mean actors are going to be paid to say those things? And people are going to pay to hear them? Don't kid yourself, people won't go to the theatre to see that! They're not crazy! Go on, take it home with you. I don't want to hear another word about it. And if you, you put it on, don't tell me . . . Especially if it's a hit . . .

> *She goes toward the door.*
> *ALEX I comes in in a dressing gown and funny*
> *slippers.*
> *MADELEINE I and CLAUDE are clearly*
> *ill-at-ease.*

ALEX I:

Jesus Christ, did somebody die around here? Come on, lighten up! I didn't come all this way for a funeral! My God, your chins are on the floor! You know me, when I get home I want a party! You can sort out your problems when I'm not here. How 'bout getting me a nice beer, Madeleine? My throat feels like sandpaper . . . And make it a cold one, the one I had in the bathtub was almost as warm as the water. Yechhh!

> *MADELEINE I goes out silently despite her son's*
> *furious expression.*

35

CLAUDE:
> For God's sake, couldn't you get it yourself?

ALEX I:
> We each have our jobs, my boy. I look after the
> money, your mother looks after the beer!

CLAUDE:
> How can you say such outrageous things, and find
> them funny?

ALEX I:
> It's a joke! You know it's a joke. I treat your mother
> like a queen, and she treats me like the prodigal son!
> It's been our little game for years, it's none of your
> concern. Especially you! If anyone's spoiled rotten
> around here, it's you!   *MADELEINE I comes back*
> *in with a bottle of beer.*   Isn't that right, Mado, you
> spoil the kids rotten?

MADELEINE I:
> When you start calling me Mado, I know you've got
> more than one warm beer in your system . . .

CLAUDE:
> See, it's not true you can't answer back . . .

ALEX I:
> Your mother? Answer back? How do you think she
> hooked me? No one could put a guy in his place like
> her! She knocked me down to size so often I figured:
> if I'm gonna take her in hand, I'll have to marry her!
> But I never succeeded. After twenty-six years of
> marriage she still has the last word!

MADELEINE I:
> I only get the last word 'cause you start snoring before
> I finish speaking!

> *She goes out.*

ALEX I: *laughing*
> Boy, is it ever good to get home . . . Every time . . .
> after all these years . . . How 'bout you, still no
> wedding bells?

> *CLAUDE sighs in exasperation.*

ALEX I:
> I'm like a broken record, eh? No one gets married
> anymore . . . You do your thing together and when it
> doesn't work . . . *adios amigos!* *He drinks.* I've
> been driving so long on bumpy roads, my arms are
> still shaking . . . even after a bath . . .

> *Silence.*

> Well, I guess I can't count on you for a sparkling
> conversation. Were you talking about me when I
> came in? I showed up a bit too early, eh? I have the
> knack of arriving at the wrong time. Always have! "I
> didn't expect you 'til tomorrow," or "I didn't expect
> you at all, I thought you were dead!"

CLAUDE:
> Must admit, you're not great for giving advance
> notice. You show up, we're all supposed to jump!

ALEX I:
> You got it, pal! And you're supposed to appreciate
> me! *He laughs.* You think I'm loud, don't you?
> I bet you don't discuss me too often with your beatnik
> friends . . .

CLAUDE:
> Beatniks went out a long time ago, Papa . . .

ALEX I:
> Not that long . . . I can still see you, in your
> turtleneck and black pants . . .

CLAUDE:
> I was eighteen . . .

ALEX I:
> Remember the time I hauled you out of the Paloma
> 'cause your mother got worried seeing you come
> home with bags under your eyes, all strung out from
> drinking too much coffee? She even thought you were
> on goofballs! Hey, her darling son was hanging out
> with a bad crowd . . . getting corrupted! I bet you
> were really ashamed of me then, eh? The travelling
> salesman father who dares interrupt the sacred
> proceedings of the enlightened few who think they're
> going to change the world. The stupid, contemptible
> working man, who barges in unannounced on the
> intellectual elite, the bearers of truth! Remember
> what I did when we left? Eh? Bought a round for the
> whole gang! I got class!

CLAUDE:
> What you don't know is that nobody gave a shit! After
> you left they all refused to drink it.

> *ALEX I gets up, furious.*

ALEX I:
> You never told me that!

CLAUDE:
> I was afraid you'd go smash the place.

ALEX I:
> You were right to be afraid, kiddo! Bunch of
> screwballs! What a lot of pissy little snobs! Is the
> Paloma still open or did some father have the brains
> to go burn it down before me?

CLAUDE:
> That's you in a nutshell, set fire to anything you don't
> understand . . .

ALEX I:
> Well, have I got a surprise for you. I'll prove I'm not
> as ignorant or as intolerant as you think. Don't look so
> stunned, I know the word intolerant. I travel, you

know . . . I'm not like the rest of you . . . I see more
than the four walls of a Montreal apartment! I mix
with people far more important and interesting than
your little gang of nobodies who think they're God's
gift to the universe!

CLAUDE:
Oh, I've no doubt you mix with people . . .

ALEX I:
Let me tell you something. I was lying there in my
bath with my gut sticking out, my beer in one hand, a
washcloth in the other, and I said to myself, I've been
unfair to you. That's right. My only son, who I used to
be so proud of—'til you went to high school anyway,
when you got all your fancy ideas—my only son
wants to become a writer and I laugh at him . . . I
ought to be proud of him . . . I can just see myself
arriving at Thetford Mines or Trois Rivières with
your first book . . . I tell you, that'd make a few
assholes pucker up with envy . . . Eh? But I said to
myself, instead of encouraging him, I put him down
before I've read a single line he's written. What if it's
good, what if I like it, you never know! We're all alike
in this family, eh? Too quick to judge . . . See, you've
told me that so often, I start to believe you . . . So, my
boy, I decided to ask the big question . . . When you
feel like showing me something you've written, any
old time, when you're ready, I'm game! How's that
grab you? I've decided to give you a fair shake . . . On
top of that, I promise I'll read it from start to finish,
the whole thing. That's a promise! But I'm warning
you, if it's boring you're gonna know about it! What
do you say to that? How's that for a father?

CLAUDE:
You'll never be serious, will you? You play the good
father, and you're so proud of yourself!

ALEX I:
Not at all, I'm very sincere!

ALEX II comes back with the phone.

ALEX II:
    What am I gonna do? I can't let them stab me in the
    back like that! Nosy bitches, they're all the same,
    sooner or later they back you into a corner! Can't hide
    a thing from them! Not a goddamn thing. I need a
    beer . . . and a good hot bath . . .

    He goes toward the kitchen.

ALEX I:
    So, what do you say?

CLAUDE: *softly*
    You've promised me so many things in my life that
    you never gave me . . . I'm sure this is one more
    you'll forget . . .

ALEX I:
    I never gave you anything?

CLAUDE:
    Hold it . . . I didn't say you never gave me
    anything . . . I said you'd . . . promised me things . . .

ALEX I:
    I always keep my promises. When did I promise you
    something I didn't deliver?

CLAUDE:
    Papa, my childhood, my adolescence, they're full of
    promises you didn't keep . . .

ALEX I:
    Oh sure, if you're gonna go back to Genesis . . .

CLAUDE:
    That's right, it's in the past, so forget it! How long is
    your memory, Papa, two weeks? Three? That's
    always been my impression.

ALEX I:

> The important things I remember . . . the rest . . .
> What do you expect, with the life I lead, if I had to
> remember everything . . .

CLAUDE:

> Okay, an example: do you remember the Police
> Youth Association?

ALEX I:

> Police Youth Association? What's that?

CLAUDE:

> You see . . . You went on about that for two years,
> Papa. Two winters in a row you promised to enroll
> me in the Police Youth Association to make a man of
> me, and I believed you. For two years. When you
> came in the door the first thing you'd say was, "Next
> Monday, my boy, put on your white shirt and your
> Sunday pants, we're off to the Police Youth
> Association. They'll make you work out, they'll make
> a man of you, they'll show you what life's all about!
> You'll forget about those books, you'll learn to sweat.
> Buckets!" So every Monday I'd drive Mama crazy 'til
> she got out my best clothes . . . except you were
> never here on Monday. You've never been here
> Mondays, that's probably why you chose that night.
> But I waited for you! Decked out in my best clothes,
> my nose glued to the window . . .

ALEX I:

> I said that to make you happy, Claude, so you'd know
> I was thinking of you, that you were important . . .
> What else could I do, I wasn't around much, I didn't
> want you to forget me . . .

CLAUDE:

> Don't worry, I didn't forget you . . . You were here so
> little I thought of nothing else! It became an
> obsession! And when Mama told us you were on your
> way home, I'd get so excited I'd have a fever! Every
> time, every time I'd wait for an explanation . . . I'd

41

have believed any lie, no matter how big, rather than admit to myself it was an empty promise . . . You'd walk in, you'd make your same friggin' promise, and you'd go take your friggin' bath! And I believed you! And I kept telling my friends: next Monday my father's taking me to the Police Youth Association, and they're going to teach me to kick the shit out of you! Of course they'd all laugh at me, but I didn't care! Each time I was sure this was it! And the following week we'd start again. You'd get out of your bath, put on your friggin' dressing gown, and not a word about the Police Youth Association. I followed you like a puppy, my heart racing, I couldn't take my eyes off you, I was practically in your lap while you were eating . . . You, you'd make your promise, you weren't even aware of me . . .

ALEX I:
Come on, don't try to tell me I ruined your life 'cause I didn't enroll you in the Police Youth Association . . .

CLAUDE:
When you pretend not to understand like that, it's so insulting . . . I give you an example, just one. Ah, forget it!

ALEX I:
Why do you bring this up all of a sudden?

CLAUDE:
Because what I write is directly related to it . . . so maybe you should read it . . .

ALEX I:
You talk about me in the stuff you write?

MADELEINE II comes in rubbing her wrist, followed by ALEX II.

ALEX II:
You worry about what goes on in the house, don't stick your nose in what happens elsewhere!

42

MADELEINE II:
> I didn't have to! What happened elsewhere came to me!

ALEX II:
> Don't talk back! I know you can answer back! Always thought you were smarter than me, eh? I know you! You watch every move I make, judge everything I say, but you don't mind taking the money I bring home, do you? Well I'm telling you, you're staying here! I didn't sweat blood raising a family to find myself twenty-five years later with a wife and kids who despise me! Or alone after a humiliating divorce!

ALEX I:
> You watch your step, my boy! You watch what you say about me! I've been patient with you, I've let a lot of things go by, but my patience has a limit! I haven't sacrificed all my life to support you and the others to find myself with a thankless kid who stabs me in the back first chance he gets! You've always looked down on me, always thought you were smarter than me, but you watch your step! If you push me far enough, and all I've got left are my fists, you'll really be sorry I didn't take you to the Police Youth Association!

ALEX II:
> It's the first time I've touched you in twenty-five years, but if that's what it takes . . .

MADELEINE II:
> It is not the first time you've touched me . . . You've got a short memory!

CLAUDE:
> You've used your fists already, don't you remember?

THE TWO ALEXES:
> That's not true . . .

ALEX II:
> I've never touched you . . .

ALEX I:
> I've never laid a hand on any of you . . .

CLAUDE:
> That's true, you're right . . . you threatened to once,
> but you didn't . . .

ALEX I:
> I threatened to more than once, and maybe I should
> have more than once. Maybe I'd get a little more
> respect around here!

ALEX II:
> When? When did I touch you?

ALEX I:
> If you're gonna start inventing things! You can hold it
> against me for the promises I made and didn't keep
> when you were small 'cause I didn't know how else
> to get you off my back, but don't make up things that
> might have consequences! I never hit you, never, so
> don't let me hear you say otherwise!

MADELEINE II:
> If you've managed to forget, good for you. It was the
> best thing you could do, I suppose . . .

ALEX II:
> I didn't manage to forget, I don't remember!

MADELEINE II:
> I'm not surprised. That's you in a nutshell. What you
> don't like, you don't see . . . or you just forget.
> Nevertheless . . . it was a horrible moment in my
> life . . .

ALEX II:
> Okay, it was a horrible moment. Christ, at this rate
> we'll have to canonize you before the night's out!

MADELEINE II:
> Alex, please, don't make jokes. It won't work, not today.

CLAUDE:
> Papa, may I ask you a question?

ALEX I:
> I don't know. To be honest, I don't know what to expect from you now.

ALEX II:
> Okay . . . look . . . what did I do that was so terrible? . . . When? . . . I honestly think if I ever raised a hand to you, I'd remember . . .

MADELEINE II:
> Once, only once in my life, I asked you to look after the kids . . .

> *ALEX II starts.*

CLAUDE:
> Remember once, when we were small, Mariette and I, Mama asked you to look after us . . .

ALEX I:
> Do I remember! Yeah, I was so bored I got plastered! 'Specially since Mariette was at least twelve or thirteen, and was old enough to babysit . . . See, I told you your mother was over-protective . . .

> *He goes out to the kitchen.*

MADELEINE II:
> Mother was dying, and the family decided we should all be with her . . .

ALEX II:
> Don't start on that! I told you, I never want to hear about that night again!

MADELEINE II:
>Because you don't want to talk about it doesn't mean
>it didn't happen, Alex . . .

ALEX II:
>It didn't happen, goddamnit! It was all in your head!
>That's what always scared me. I saw something in
>your eyes that night I'd never seen before and . . .
>You're right, I decided to forget it! Okay, I admit I'd
>forgotten some of it! But I don't want to talk about it
>now any more than I did then . . .

MADELEINE II:
>I also saw things in your eyes that night, Alex, things
>I'd never seen before! But I could never forget them,
>even if I spent the rest of my life trying!

ALEX II:
>If you ask me, you've made a point of not forgetting!
>'Specially since nothing happened that night, and you
>know it!

>*He grabs her by the wrist.*

ALEX II:
>If something had really happened that night, you'd
>have taken the kids and left. Your accusations were
>so horrible, you'd never have wanted to see me again!
>The proof that nothing happened is that you stayed!

MADELEINE II:
>I stayed because I had no place to go . . .

ALEX II:
>You stayed because you knew you'd imagined it! It's
>true I hit you that night, I remember very well . . .
>Yeah, I smacked you one, and you know what? You
>deserved it! You drag it up again tonight 'cause you
>think you're gonna dump me, and it suits you to keep
>finding reasons to do it! I'm not blind, you know . . .
>You're a goddamn hypocrite and you know it!

Silence.
MADELEINE II goes up to her husband and looks
him straight in the eye.

MADELEINE II:
Mariette told me everything that night. A child of
thirteen doesn't lie about those things! If you don't
want to discuss it, that's fine. I think I'd prefer it that
way myself. But I want you to know once and for all
that I've always known, and if I never said anything
it's because I was afraid. A man who can do things
like that is capable of anything . . .

ALEX I returns with his beer.

CLAUDE:
You remember what happened that night?

ALEX I sits in an armchair.

MADELEINE II:
Have you ever felt you've been buried under a ton of
bricks? Or hit over the head with a hammer? Because
in a split second your whole life got changed? One
moment, you're someone with a certain frame of
mind . . . you're sure you know who you are and who
the others are around you . . . You don't question
anything about them . . . haven't for ages. Your
world . . . is definitive. My world was definitive,
Alex. I had . . . arrived somewhere . . . for good. I
understood everything that had happened to me. I
even had . . . a grip on my most serious problems . . .
which weren't really all that bad, but could have kept
me from being happy if I hadn't had them in hand . . .
Mother's death shook me up, that's certain, but we'd
all expected it and I knew I'd get over it . . . That
evening, I came home from her place . . . at peace
with myself. I'd done my duty, mother had talked to
me, I'd managed to calm her down a bit, she was so
scared of dying . . . It's hard to explain . . . When I
climbed the stairs I was someone very precise . . .
and when I opened the door I became someone

else . . . At that exact moment I was forced to become someone else . . . because all of a sudden my whole life collapsed around me. It was as if I'd entered into someone else's skin . . . and it wasn't even someone I wanted to know. With no warning I was forced to jump from one life to another. My husband, my children, had changed while I was away. I'd left a perfectly happy and quiet household and all of a sudden I landed back in some kind of . . . incomprehensible hell. When you hit me, I didn't even feel it. It wasn't me you hit, it was the other one . . . the unhappy woman I still didn't know . . . I couldn't even hate you right away, I had so little notion of what was happening . . . *She looks at ALEX II.* But since then I've had time to catch up, though I've never been able to tell you . . . rather I've let the chances go by . . . out of . . . fear probably . . . Ever since then I've been afraid of you, Alex . . . But today it's my turn to make you change your world. When you came through that door a while ago, you entered another world. How does it feel? *ALEX II doesn't answer. MADELEINE II shrugs her shoulders and goes out.*

ALEX I:
Nothing happened. I watched the hockey game, you whined all night 'cause you couldn't stand it, and Mariette sulked 'cause I wouldn't let her go out . . . Why do you want to know? You're not still on about whether or not I hit you? I no more hit anyone that night than any other!

MARIETTE I bursts in.

MARIETTE I:
My favourite Papa!

ALEX I:
My favourite daughter!

They throw themselves in each other's arms. CLAUDE is ill-at-ease.

48

ALEX I:
> You're just in time! Your brother's giving me the third degree about something that happened before the flood!

MARIETTE I:
> That's how he gets his kicks these days . . . Hi, little brother . . . Still picking at old wounds? The last six weeks, he hasn't let me alone either . . . He's got an incredible memory, you know. He's been telling me stuff I'd forgotten since I was a kid!

ALEX I:
> Yeah, and if you ask me, he's getting dangerous.

> > *MARIETTE II comes in, closing her umbrella. She sees her father on the sofa.*
> > *She leans against the door frame.*

MARIETTE II:
> Are you examining your conscience?

> > *ALEX II jumps.*

ALEX II:
> You scared me . . .

> > *She comes into the living room, removing her raincoat.*

ALEX I:
> How're ya doin', Baby-doll?

MARIETTE I:
> A-one! Bone tired, 'cause I've been working too hard, but, you know, when you're tired like that, it makes you feel good . . .

ALEX I:
> Still kicking up your heels?

MARIETTE I:
>It's all I know how to do! That and things you don't
tell your papa . . .

>*They laugh.*

MARIETTE II:
>Mama was pretty worried . . . you should phone
when you know you're gonna be a few days late . . .

ALEX II:
>I don't know when I'm gonna be late . . .

MARIETTE II:
>Doesn't cost much to phone . . .

ALEX II:
>Sometimes I don't want to listen to her
complaints . . . Calling here is like punching the
clock! I chose a line of work where I'd be free to move
around 'cause I didn't want to be cooped up in a
factory all my life. Your mother knows that, I've told
her a thousand times . . . I like my freedom!

ALEX I:
>I saw you on T.V. the other night . . . Thanks for
calling to let me know . . . I tell you, that made 'em
drool . . . Hey, my daughter on T.V . . . They
couldn't believe it . . . neither could I . . . We got a
good shot of you, too . . . Not for long, but we
recognized you . . . Too bad colour T.V. isn't here yet.

MARIETTE I:
>Looks like I'll be on even more next time . . . Hey,
did you know I was one of the first gogo dancers in
Montreal? . . . I got experience! I show the others
how to do it . . .

ALEX I:
>You sure know how to shake it. You should have seen
the guys at Hotel Lapointe . . .

MARIETTE I:
> You should see the studio technicians! Boy, do we
> have fun . . . You know, if this keeps up I won't have
> to dance in the clubs all the time . . .

MARIETTE II:
> Speaking of freedom . . . was that a coincidence the
> other night?

ALEX II:
> The other night . . .

MARIETTE II:
> Papa, don't play dumb! The other night, the Hotel
> Rancourt in Victoriaville!

ALEX II:
> Oh, yeah . . . yeah, that was a coincidence . . .

ALEX I:
> You can make your living on television?

MARIETTE I:
> No, but with television I can slack off a bit . . . It's not
> easy, you know, climbing into that cage every night
> and wiggling your ass for hours . . . It's not
> something casual I do to relax . . . It's work, I do it
> every night! Hardly ever in the same place! Some of
> the dumps I see . . . you wouldn't believe me if I told
> you . . .

ALEX I:
> Mariette . . . I travel too, you know!

MARIETTE I:
> Yeah, I guess you see some doozers too . . . But you
> never talk about them . . . You never tell us your
> adventures on the highroads of Quebec . . . I have a
> sneaking suspicion that some of them aren't too
> tellable . . . you're such a rascal . . .

ALEX II:
I didn't even know you were in the area . . . I just happened to go in . . .

MARIETTE II:
And you just happened to be with six of your salesman friends . . .

ALEX II:
Mariette . . . Saturday nights, we often get together for a drink . . .

MARIETTE I:
I bet Claude would love to hear them . . . wouldn't you, Claude? Boy, the questions you'd ask Mama to find out what Papa does on his weekends . . .

ALEX II:
We all know where to find each other. We leave messages . . .

CLAUDE:
Didn't you want to know?

MARIETTE I:
Sure, but I didn't bug Mama about it . . .

MARIETTE II:
And once a month you just happen to stumble on a hotel where I'm working!

CLAUDE:
No, knowing you, you'd go directly to him . . .

MARIETTE I:
Look who's jealous . . .

CLAUDE:
I'm not jealous!

ALEX I:
> Leave him be, he's in a bad mood today . . . Don't
> bother him, he bites!

> *They laugh.*

MARIETTE II:
> Look, while we're alone . . . there's something I want
> to ask you . . . It's embarrassing, Papa, to dance on a
> stage when you know you're father's watching . . .

ALEX II:
> For Chrissake, you're not doing a striptease!

MARIETTE II:
> You shout louder than the others, you clap louder . . .
> You and your buddies aren't too subtle, Papa . . . I
> don't know . . . it's unhealthy . . .

ALEX II:
> Unhealthy! What's unhealthy?

MARIETTE II:
> Papa, it's as if you're selling me! There you are,
> following me around month after month with a
> bunch of drunks . . . The hotel managers have started
> calling you my fan club . . . Good thing they don't
> know you're my father! Put yourself in my place!
> There I am busting my ass on stage to get people to
> dance and drink, and I know my own father's out
> there making jokes with a bunch of pigs who think
> I'm just a piece of meat!

ALEX II:
> If you can't handle it, find another job!

MARIETTE II:
> I can handle it! I've been doing it long enough! But
> not in front of my father! Can't you understand?

MARIETTE I:
Ah, well . . . Before he was just jealous, now he's
ashamed too . . .

CLAUDE:
Great . . . here we go . . .

MARIETTE I:
I'll bet you weren't glued to the T.V. the other night
when your gogo girl sister made her debut!

CLAUDE:
No, you're right, but that doesn't mean I'm
ashamed . . . That kind of show doesn't interest me,
that's all . . . And I sure wouldn't watch it just 'cause
my sister's making a fool of herself locked up in some
cage, dancing like a monkey in a mini-skirt!

MARIETTE II:
I can see your eyes, you know . . . Yours as much as
the others'!

CLAUDE:
Sorry. I sound like a shit, I don't mean that . . .

MARIETTE I:
Oh, yes you do . . .

ALEX II:
What's wrong with my eyes . . .

MARIETTE II:
They're ugly! Like the others'!

MARIETTE I:
You and your snooty airs, you can't fool me . . .
You've always spied on me, you've always twisted
everything I said and did. When you were a kid you
were always snooping around, minding other
peoples' business. We never knew where you were.
You were always creeping around behind some
armchair or hiding in a closet . . . You spent your

childhood spying on us! You wouldn't say a word for
days, but we knew you'd listened to everything we'd
said.   *She sighs in exasperation.*   Ah, why am I
saying all this? I was in a good mood when I came
in . . .

ALEX I:
  'Course you were, now relax . . . How 'bout a beer
  with your old man . . . We haven't seen each other
  for weeks . . .

MARIETTE I:
  You know he came all the way up to Shawinigan to
  ask me questions . . . I don't know what stage he's
  going through, but boy, is he weird . . . He wanted to
  know what happened one night when you babysat us,
  when Grandma was dying . . . Can you remember
  that?

ALEX I:
  Jesus-Christ, he's got a one-track mind! You bet I
  remember, I'd never babysat before and I thought I'd
  go nuts . . . You were a giant pain, the pair of you . . .
  You, you wouldn't go to sleep unless I sat beside your
  bed and held your hand . . . You sulked for hours
  when I wouldn't let you go out, then you wouldn't let
  me leave you alone . . . I think I fell asleep too . . .
  Too much beer . . .

CLAUDE:
  Yeah, that's always been your version . . .

MARIETTE II:
  Look, I'm not accusing you . . . but when you've had
  lots to drink and heard lots of jokes about me . . .
  don't you forget sometimes I'm your daughter?

ALEX II:
  What do you mean?

MARIETTE II:
  Well, you did forget once . . .

CLAUDE:
And we all chose to believe it . . .

ALEX I laughs.

ALEX I:
Claude, I can't believe you would think . . .

MARIETTE I:
You must be sick!

ALEX II:
Okay, so I forgot once! Okay!

MARIETTE I:
You're sick in the head!

ALEX II:
But it was no big deal . . . I stopped in time . . .

MARIETTE II:
That's not true! If Claude hadn't come in . . .

ALEX I:
Jesus-Christ! All this time you've been thinking that of me!

CLAUDE:
You'd been playing around with each other, for some time . . .

MARIETTE II:
You'd been playing around with me for some time . . . 'Course we'd always done that . . .

MARIETTE I:
Maybe so, but Claude, we always did that . . . Papa played with you too! He did that with everyone . . . I'm sure he still does it, even if it's not with us anymore . . . He's a touchy-feely guy, that's all! It's not a disease!

MARIETTE II:
Of course it was nice when I was a kid . . . My father
was different from the others . . . He wasn't just
funny, he was loveable! We were always kissing and
holding hands . . . You'd sweet-talk me so much I'd
get goose-bumps . . . I'd kiss you on the ear and you'd
tell me you could feel it to the tips of your toes . . .

MARIETTE I:
It's true, for a while there it bothered me, but . . .

MARIETTE II:
Naturally I liked it . . . You were like Santa Claus . . .
We hardly ever saw you, so when you came home
you were . . . superimportant. Everything was
different, nothing else counted . . . you were the
centre of everything . . .

MARIETTE I:
Do you remember when I started to fill out . . . I was
so embarrassed, I tried to hide it but they wouldn't go
away . . . You, when you came home that time, you
wouldn't let up! I was so ashamed! You pulled out all
your farmer's daughter jokes, I thought I'd die! I even
asked Mama to buy me an old lady's nightgown, and I
wore it around the house hoping nothing would
show . . . Talk about naive! One thing's for sure, I
didn't let you play with me then . . . nor the next
time . . . No more horsing around, eh! I left that to
Claude, who kept himself quite busy, if I
remember . . . Anyway, I was so embarrassed by the
changes that were happening in me, I could hardly
look you guys in the face . . .

She laughs.

MARIETTE I:
I could talk about it with my friends, that was
easy . . . but with you . . . and even with Mama, it
was impossible . . . I was a big girl, and that was
it . . . Oh, she'd explained it, all the physical stuff . . .
but it made no difference! Now, when I think back on

that time . . . I miss it . . . even if I was miserable . . .
It's nice to think those things made me blush . . . I
miss being dumb and naive . . . sometimes I wish I
still were.

MARIETTE II:
But it wasn't so nice when I became a woman . . . I
changed . . . and so did you. You didn't look at me
the same way any more . . . Oh, you were still funny,
still a Santa Claus, but there was something new that
made me uneasy . . . I'd catch you staring at me
without saying anything . . . It gave me the
creeps . . . Your kisses . . . were more insistent . . .
your jokes more pointed . . . your compliments more
embarrassing. Mama began telling you not to play
with me so much . . . I wasn't sure why, but
something told me she was right. So you horsed
around with Claude, halfheartedly. You never paid
him much attention, did you? Sometimes we thought
it was because you weren't interested in the same
things . . . You even laughed at him, at his books and
T.V. shows you thought were stupid . . . Anyway,
you were still buzzing around me without . . . getting
too close . . . until that night . . .

ALEX II:
Don't talk about that. It's a dead issue, I've sorted it
out.

MARIETTE II:
You've sorted it out, that's all that counts! What
happened to me doesn't matter!

MARIETTE I:
You know what? When you came and lay down
beside me that night, everything felt right again . . . I
had my old papa, and that made me feel good. Santa
was back.

ALEX I: *to CLAUDE*
You see?

MARIETTE I:
That was the last time in my life I felt like a little girl.
It was sort of a turning point. I fell asleep too, I
think . . . like you . . . But then snoopy here turned
up! The cries, the tears, the drama . . . Poor Mama
comes running in, she doesn't know what's
happened . . . we must have woken the whole bloody
neighbourhood! I was hysterical, I was bawling like a
baby . . . and the whole thing ended in a horrible
misunderstanding . . . *to Claude* Thanks to
you . . .

MARIETTE II:
Your smell of beer, your crazy eyes . . . Not much
like Santa, that's for sure! Can you imagine what it's
like for a young girl to see her father in that state? I
tried to tell myself you'd been drinking, you were
angry at me 'cause I'd been bad, you didn't know
what you were doing . . . There are no explanations,
Papa, no excuses! That cuts a life in two! It breaks . . .
something for ever! It destroyed everything I felt for
you . . . all the admiration . . . the love. Just like that.
In that one night, I grew older. And you . . . you died.
Then Claude came in, just in time, and all hell broke
loose . . . He was probably jealous, but never
mind . . . it saved me . . . literally . . . Because if he
hadn't come in . . . and if Mama hadn't arrived and
stood up for us . . . We both saw you hit her, Papa,
because she knew what was going to happen! You hit
her because you were about to do something
monstrous! Instead of punishing yourself, you
punished her! Someone else always pays, don't they!
You can't face yourself, so you punish others! *She
comes very close to her father.* And I relive the
whole thing when you come to see me dance! That's
exactly how I feel! I can see you, you know. The stage
isn't so bright I can't see you, you and your friends!
And the way you look at me, there's no difference
between you and them. None! How do explain it to
them, what you're doing, how can you look them in
the face? Or is that part of the trip? Does it turn them
on, knowing you're gonna watch your own daughter

dance in every sleazy hotel in the province? You can't answer. You really don't want to talk about it, do you?

MARIETTE I: *to CLAUDE*
Is that clear enough for you? Does it satisfy your sick curiosity? What you thought was monstrous was nothing at all . . .

ALEX II:
I've had to live with that . . . ever since, Mariette! You understand . . . if I have to talk about it too . . .

MARIETTE II:
It might do you good.

ALEX II:
To forget will do me good. Nothing more. Nothing less.

MARIETTE II:
Fine, so forget me! I came to ask you . . . no, not to ask . . . I came to tell you, never come to see me dance again, Papa! You hear? If you ever set foot in a club where I'm dancing, I'll do something you'll never forget! After that, those pigs you call friends won't give you the time of day! You'll be branded for life! I'm through being humiliated by you when I'm trying to work, now it'll be your turn!   *She picks up her umbrella and raincoat.*   Tell Mama I came by to pick up my umbrella and couldn't stay 'cause my taxi was waiting . . .

She leaves.

ALEX II:
I don't take orders from you! My Saturday nights are mine and I'll do what I fucking please! Neither of you broads will change a thing in my life, okay!

He finishes his beer.

ALEX I: *to CLAUDE*
I see now, I should have given you the thrashing you
deserved that night . . . Might have knocked some
sense into you. Instead of making up lies, inventing
stories, why didn't you come and see me? You prefer
your own version, eh? Is that it? It's more exciting to
imagine something happened! And then drag it
around for years! Well, if that's your image of me,
kiddo . . .

CLAUDE:
It's always the same around here. If anything serious
happens, it ends up having no importance because
you all prefer it that way! How many laundered
versions of things have I heard? I know I can't win
against you . . . maybe that's why I do something else
with what happened here . . .

MARIETTE I:
You still think you're right?

CLAUDE:
I don't know if I'm right. I'm searching . . .

ALEX I:
Don't search too hard! Things may be a lot simpler
than what's in your head . . .

CLAUDE:
Maybe they're more complicated than you'd care to
admit!

ALEX II:
Why is everything so complicated?

MARIETTE I approaches her brother.

MARIETTE I:

Complicate your life all you want, but leave us out of
it. All of us. Okay? Do your snooping elsewhere,
maybe it'll smell worse, the way you like it . . .
Here . . . it just smells normal . . . That's not
interesting . . . We're not interesting enough for you,
Claude . . . We're not sick enough . . .

She leaves.

ALEX II:

It was so simple the way it was. So simple. When I
was small, my mother always said: ''You can never
get home scott free.'' I thought she was crazy. And all
my life I've tried to prove her wrong. I've busted my
ass to hang on to my freedom, and I'll be damned if
I'm gonna lose it! Why should I pay now for stuff that
happened ages ago? I'm not gonna pay! I won't!
They'll take me as I am, like it or lump it! Who's boss
around here, eh? I'm not gonna be led around by the
nose! Not by some hysterical cow who doesn't know
what she's saying, nor by some gogo dancer who
doesn't want people to see her dance! I'll see her
dance all I want. If she wants to show off her tits, let
her show 'em! It's good for business. My pals envy
me, so do my clients! And when I watch her, I'll think
what I like!

He drinks.

ALEX II:

You bring up a kid . . . a little doll you can play with
all you want . . . You can kiss her on her bum, her
tummy, kiss her little mouth, tickle her . . . For years
you can do what you like with her, it's just a game,
just for fun, it's daddy and his little girl having
fun . . . You see her growing up, sometimes so fast it
worries you, but no big deal, she's still your baby girl
and you go on tossing her in the air, pretending you
won't catch her, to give her a scare so she'll hug you a
little harder . . . Then one day . . . the conspiracy
begins . . . the conspiracy of women . . . It starts with

whispers in the hallway . . . You think they're talking behind your back . . . hiding something from you . . . something you should know, but they don't want to tell you . . . and your little girl's not as cuddly either . . . suddenly she's modest . . . blushes more easily . . . You want to keep playing, but your baby, who's changing before your very eyes, hesitates, runs away, she finds excuses for not coming too close . . . Christ, it's almost like being jilted! You think she's turned her back on you because you've done something, and you don't know what! Then one day you manage to get her on the sofa . . . You were so happy, it was the first time in ages! After a few cuddles, just like the old days, you feel . . . you too, for the first time . . . you feel that something's changed . . . Not just in her eyes . . . Her body . . . Beneath her blouse . . . And it all comes clear. The conspiracy! If she's afraid of you, it's got to be her mother who's told her that now she's a big girl she mustn't touch her father any more! So it's them! It's the women. They put those ideas in your head! You just wanted your child to stay a child, but they put something else in your head, that if you feel like it . . . Well, I felt like it! It's too bad, but I felt like it! And . . . I still do!

He finishes his beer.

I'm thirsty . . . I'm thirsty! I want a beer! I want someone to get me a beer! It's my house, I paid for it, I paid for everything, it's all mine, and I want a beer!

MADELEINE I comes in.

MADELEINE I:
Dinner's served. Come and sit down. But I want to talk to Claude first.   *to ALEX I*   Go sit down, Mariette's already there . . . I'll be right in.

He goes out.

63

ALEX II:
I want a beer!

MADELEINE I jumps.
Silence.
MADELEINE II enters the room.
She is holding ALEX II's suitcase in one hand, and a
beer in the other.

MADELEINE II:
Here! Here's your beer. But it's your last. And the
pleasure's all mine.

ALEX II:
What do you mean, my last?

MADELEINE II:
Don't play dumb. No point your staying here tonight,
eh? Things might get out of hand. The mere thought
of you in this house kills me, Alex.

MADELEINE I takes CLAUDE's manuscript and
hands it to him.

MADELEINE I:
I don't want you to stay for supper tonight . . . I'm
not throwing you out, I'm just asking you not to
stay . . . I'd feel you were spying on us again, I
wouldn't be able to talk, I'd be anxious about
everything your father said . . . I don't think I can
ever be natural again with you, Claude . . .   *She*
goes towards the kitchen door.   And don't call. Wait
to hear from me.

She leaves.

ALEX II:
You think you can toss me out?

MADELEINE II:
> You bet I do. I've had it! I've put up with enough,
> swallowed enough, I'm through tearing myself to
> pieces . . . I'm tired of telling myself I'm wrong about
> you, that deep down you're a good guy who's just not
> too bright and not very responsible . . . I'm fed up.
> I've had enough. If you don't leave, I will . . .

ALEX II:
> You're not leaving. And neither am I. Things will stay
> as they are, okay!

MADELEINE II:
> Be careful, Alex. I've always been gentle and
> understanding, but there's a whole other side of me
> you don't know. Everyone has a hidden side, you're
> not the only one who can fool people. So watch out
> for what you don't know about me.

ALEX II:
> Threats?

MADELEINE II:
> I suppose you could call it that. It makes me feel good
> to know I can threaten you, Alex! I see a flicker of
> doubt in your eyes, and I like it . . . I think you're
> really getting scared . . . Your view of things is
> changing, eh? It's not as clear as it was . . . Well, what
> you see now is nothing compared with what you'd
> see if I let myself go! I've got twenty-five years of
> frustration inside me, Alex, and I hope for your sake
> it doesn't all come out at once. Believe me, you'd be a
> lot smarter to find a hotel tonight . . . It'll save
> you . . . a lot of cruel words, some unpleasant
> surprises, and some devastating insults. But if you
> prefer, if you insist, if you choose to stay, I'm ready to
> face you, tell you everything. Everything. I can do
> amazing things tonight, Alex; I can also save you from
> them. I'll give you time to choose . . . time enough for
> a beer which, in any case, is your last. When I come
> back, if you're still here, watch out.

We hear the third movement of Mendelsohn's fifth symphony. MADELEINE II slowly goes up to CLAUDE and taps him on the shoulder as if to say "good work."
She in turn goes out.
CLAUDE and ALEX II are alone on stage.
ALEX II puts his head in his hands.
CLAUDE hugs his manuscript.

ALEX II: *straightening up*
If there's nothing left for me, there'll be nothing for you either.

> *Very deliberately, he trashes the living room. He leaves.*

> *ALEX I enters slowly, goes up to CLAUDE and takes the manuscript out of his hands.*

ALEX I:
Is this the only one, or are there copies?

CLAUDE:
It's my only one.

ALEX II:
That's risky.

CLAUDE:
I know. But I haven't had time. One of my friends said she'd give me stencils . . . I've got other things to do, you know. I've got a job, I have to earn a living too . . . I wrote this at work, in my spare time; on the corner of my boss's desk when he wasn't there; at home, nights, instead of going out . . . weekends . . .

ALEX I:
I see, a hobby . . .

CLAUDE: *sharply*
It's a lot more than a hobby, and you know it!

ALEX I:
No, I don't know. I don't know much of anything about you . . .

He leafs through the manuscript.

CLAUDE:
There's not much about me that's ever interested you . . .

ALEX I:
You're repeating yourself . . .

CLAUDE:
Not enough, maybe . . .

ALEX I:
So if I tore it up right now, if I set fire to it, it would disappear completely . . . It wouldn't exist anymore . . .

CLAUDE looks at him for a few seconds.

CLAUDE:
Are you trying to frighten me?

ALEX I:
Yep. If I were you I'd be afraid. A crazy father who doesn't want his kid to talk about him in his ''works'' . . .

CLAUDE:
As long as you're making fun of me, I know you won't do anything . . .

ALEX II throws the manuscript in the air. The pages fly all over the room. CLAUDE doesn't react.

ALEX I:
Now are you scared?

CLAUDE:
No.

ALEX I picks up a page at random.

ALEX I:
"Alex: What am I gonna do? I can't let them stab me in the back like that . . . Nosy bitches, they're all the same, sooner or later they back you into a corner!" What am I talking about? Your mother and sister? Or women in general?

He crumples up the page, tosses it across the room.

ALEX I:
Anyway, you've no right to use my name.

CLAUDE:
I already talked to Mama about that . . . I'm changing the names . . .

ALEX I:
There's the problem . . . You've always talked to your mother . . .

CLAUDE:
You were never here . . .

ALEX I:
Don't give me that Police Youth Association crap! You and your mother have been carrying on behind my back over more important things than that.

He comes over to CLAUDE and sits down beside him on the sofa.

ALEX I:
Come on, shoot. Now's the time. Let's hear everything you've got against me, I'm all ears. Unless of course you've worked it all out with your mother . . . I was too polite to listen to what you were saying earlier, but maybe I should have. Now there's

a fault I don't have: I don't eavesdrop! That must disappoint you! Come on, I don't feel like reading your great literature anymore, it might make me sick, so tell it to me, we'll have a good laugh . . .

CLAUDE:
You've always been good at defusing an important conversation . . . How do you expect us to talk seriously . . . You're already making light of everything we might say . . .

> *ALEX I almost jumps on his son, grabbing him by the collar.*

ALEX I:
I take none of this lightly, okay?

> *They look at each other a few seconds.*
> *ALEX I moves away from CLAUDE.*

ALEX I:
You like that better? The brute instead of the joker? Isn't that how you've always seen me? . . . You think I have to read that to know what you think of me? Come off it! If you needed therapy so bad, instead of tearing your heart out writing bullshit about me, why didn't you come and see me on one of my rounds? One weekend in a hotel room in Saint-Jérôme, we could have straightened this out . . . a long time ago, too . . .

CLAUDE:
That's where you're wrong . . . All you'd have straightened out is your side of things! As usual. You'd have put on a non-stop show for two days, a clever but endless monologue, mildly amusing and totally egocentric . . . You wouldn't have known I was there . . . Are you ever aware of other people when you talk? Do you ever answer their questions, wait for their answers? It's not conversations you have, it's spectacular monologues! Are you all the same, you and your buddies? Do you talk in

monologues instead of listening to each other? When you're together in Saint-Jérôme, for instance, do you all talk at the same time?

ALEX I:
Where do you get this crap? . . . You never came to Saint-Jérôme, you never wanted to. How can you guess, much less judge, what goes on there?

CLAUDE picks up several pages and waves them under his father's nose.

CLAUDE:
Do you know how long I've worked on this? How many years? With my imagination, that's right, with what I could guess about you? Do you know it's because of you I began to write? And because you always acted as if you were deaf? The first time I put a pencil to paper, I was eleven, maybe twelve, it was to talk to you 'cause I couldn't reach you, it was to tell you I loved you 'cause you probably would have slugged me if I'd actually said it . . . There were so many things we couldn't talk about in this house, I had to put them on paper or suffocate! It was my only outlet, and it gave me as much release as when I first started to masturbate! And writing made me feel just as guilty afterwards because it seemed even more forbidden! "Speaking to one's father is absolutely forbidden under pain of mortal sin, irremediable and irrevocable!" I struggled for hours trying to paint an idyllic picture of you, I described you as I wanted you to be . . . here! Just as funny, just as lively, but HERE! I didn't tear my heart out, not at all, on the contrary . . . I was so exhilarated by what I wrote, I'd nearly faint! I discovered the exhilaration of writing by making declarations of love to my father who didn't want to know about me!

ALEX I:
Shit, I left my smokes in the kitchen . . .

CLAUDE:
See , you don't want to listen! Even though you asked!

ALEX I:
You're starting again, just like when you were a kid . . . you're starting again! Clinging, saying things nobody wants to hear!

CLAUDE:
What things? What things? Name them. Come on, see if you can name them!

ALEX I:
Feelings! Feelings! I always ran away from you; I fled, 'cause it always comes back to that!

CLAUDE:
Why shouldn't it come back to that? What prevented us? Was there some rule, some law?   *ALEX I starts to get up.*   Don't run away. For once, please, don't run away . . .

ALEX I:
It's the way I am, that's all . . . I've never talked about my feelings . . . to anyone . . . and I'm not gonna start now.   *He looks his son in the eye.* Surely you could have guessed, behind the clown routines, the travelling salesman jokes . . . surely you could have guessed that behind all that there were feelings! Because I don't talk about them doesn't mean they're not there! If they don't want to come out, they won't. Don't make it a tragedy!

CLAUDE:
A child can't live on guesses! Or silence! We were often on the verge of saying things, Papa, but it never happened! We horsed around a lot, oh, did we ever, tickling each other, charging all over the house, exhausting ourselves playing hide and seek, but when we were all out of breath and we'd look each other in the eye like we are now, when something truly important might have happened between us . . .

ALEX I:
I can't, that's all! I can't! Don't ask me anymore!

CLAUDE:
Don't worry, I won't. I don't ask you for anything now. *He picks up a page.* I'm just telling you why "this" exists. When you can't talk, things have to come out some other way.

ALEX I:
Fine, now we've got something important. Let's talk about how it came out. You say when you were small, you had this idyllic picture of me. Something tells me that "this," as you say, is none too idyllic! Your image of me has changed in ten years, eh? Something tells me there's not much left of "Papa, I love you, my wonderful papa!"

CLAUDE:
Believe it or not, understanding comes with age.

ALEX I:
Understanding! Of what? I didn't become a monster between 1955 and 1965!

CLAUDE:
True, you haven't changed much. I wonder if it's normal for a human being to change so little in ten years.

ALEX I:
There . . . more contempt.

CLAUDE:
That's right . . . contempt. That's the word. I've gone from blind admiration to utter contempt . . . little by little, step by step . . . When you're a child and you *want* to admire someone, there's no fault, no blemish, no vice that can cloud your determination to admire . . . A hero's a hero, once and for always! It's absolute, incredibly inspiring! And nourishing! But as you get older . . . you change, of course. And you

72

wanted to change, to be more like him, your perfect hero who helped you through the difficulties of childhood, the problems of adolescence . . . But your hero, he stays the same, on his pedestal . . . How pathetic! Your childhood and your hero crumble at the same time. At the same time you discover the cracks in your hero and the naiveté of your childhood . . . You could die of shame . . . for having been wrong. *Silence.* You continue to grow, and you watch the cracks widen until your hero is so grotesque, you say: is that what I admired? And they say we get the heroes we deserve . . . *Silence.* I hope no one ever deserved you. *He picks up a few more sheets of paper.* I really have put all my contempt for you into this. All my . . . contempt. There's no other word. It's all there, your spinelessness, your intellectual laziness . . . your incredible intellectual laziness. You don't even know intelligence exists, that it can be used. You've never been interested in anything in your life! Or anyone. You've been totally egotistical and egocentric. It's not even a question of being mean . . . it's just unthinking selfishness . . . To be mean, you have to be conscious, use your intelligence! That's why you're so impenetrable. We can't even scratch you, others' nails don't exist for you! Your only consideration is for yourself, others can sort out their own problems . . . yours too, while they're at it. For instance, when I realized Madame Cantin in Sorel was no more important than the rest of us, and we were no more important than her and her kid, my jealousy evaporated. And God knows I was jealous . . . Hey, a second family, rivals! Thieves! Even though you were never here, I was still jealous because they stole you! Don't look at me like that, we all know about Madame Cantin, even if we never mentioned it. How's that for family solidarity . . . Well, I realized then and there how little people mean to you . . . You're totally irresponsible . . . All that matters is your beer on Saturday night, broads, a quick lay in a sleazy motel, jokes, jokes and more jokes. Papa, all you really care about is jokes! And that is contemptible. All you've changed is your jokes. You've become a great, truly great, teller of dirty jokes, nothing more, because nothing else in life interests you. Isn't that pathetic. Not an ounce of curiosity. Not a question. Nothing. You've plied the roads of Quebec all your life, building up an absurd repertoire of dirty jokes without ever asking yourself a single question! You've raised tons of dust with generations of cars on roads that weren't yet paved, and that's all you've done with your life. How can I not crucify you with my contempt? And in my play I put all that contempt into Mama's character . . . It's Mama who tells you what I think of you because she's probably the one who's suffered most from what you've been. *Ironically:* I did what you'd call . . . a transfer. That's my role . . . I guess. To have others say what they're incapable of saying, and what I can't say either. But now I'm not sure. After tonight I'm not so sure. I'm not sure I have the right to become a writer. Now I'm afraid of becoming as manipulative as you. I'm afraid of becoming a joke teller like you. Of giving birth to a string of jokes that are more and more tedious, and especially, insignificant. Tear up my play if you like, Papa, set fire to it, it's full of . . . *Silence.* Lies. Using lies I tried to tell the truth. To a certain extent I think I succeeded. I think what I wrote is good. But what's the point. What's the point, Papa, if I can't get into your heart? What's the point if you refuse to admit you have one? Look, mine's scattered all over the place, you can trample it all you want.

He goes toward the door. He turns before going out.

CLAUDE:

If I hadn't come in that night, Papa, I know you would have raped Mariette, and that too would have become a taboo subject in this house, like Madame Cantin. We would all have been . . . accomplices, once again. If no one denounces you, what will become of all of us?

He goes out.

ALEX I: *Ironically.*
Don't forget to thank me. If it's true, you owe it to me, your great writer's talent. Fucking little intellectual! That's how you've always thought of us, eh? You and your gang!

ALEX I picks up a few sheets of the manuscript and starts to burn them, one by one.

Blackout.